TEACHER
Bible Readers Series

A Study of Proverbs

FINDING THE WAY OF LIFE

Walter B. Phelps

Abingdon Press / Nashville

Finding the Way of Life
A Study of Proverbs

ISBN 0-687-05143-6

02 03 04 05 06 07 08 09 10 11—10 9 8 7 6 5 4 3 2 1
Manufactured in the United States of America.

CONTENTS

Wisdom Sayings *5*

1. The Beginning of Knowledge *7*

2. The Priority of Wisdom *13*

3. The Value of Wisdom *19*

4. Lessons From Life *23*

5. Proverbs in Pictures *27*

WISDOM SAYINGS

BY PERRY H. BIDDLE, JR.

The word for proverb in Hebrew comes from a verb meaning to be like or to compare. A proverb is a saying, usually brief but sometimes longer, that in colorful language expresses a bit of wisdom or advice. The Book of Proverbs contains such sayings, but proverbs are present in other books of the Bible also.

Our Book of Proverbs is the product of the wisdom movement in ancient Israel. King Solomon has been regarded as the official founder of Israel's wisdom movement, and he served as its patron in many ways. The Book of Proverbs is a composite book with proverbs drawn from many writers, however. This book is a compilation of originally independent, though related, collections of maxims, observations, and discourses.

Scholars suggest the fifth or fourth century B.C. as the time when the Book of Proverbs was taking shape. Some of the proverbs are closely related to the wisdom literature of ancient Egypt, however, and go back as far as the third millennium B.C. The Egyptian wisdom movement flourished in the royal court. The sayings were used in teaching the sons of the nobility so that they would be prepared for their future role as leaders of the nation.

During the period of the monarchy in Israel, a similar use was made of the proverbs (1 Kings 4:29-34). Notice that Proverbs 25:1 indicates that a number of the proverbs were copied by the men of King Hezekiah of Judah. Although proverbs were originally spoken, they eventually were written.

While the wisdom movement originally had as its function the education of the young sons of nobles for cultural and political leadership, in Israel this task was expanded to include a concern to say in human terms what the ultimate meaning of life is. What is the goal of human life, and how can people achieve that goal? The movement dealt not only with practical ethics but also with religious and theological issues. This aspect of Israel's wisdom movement is what made it more highly developed than that of Egypt or other Near Eastern countries.

A clue to the fact that the Book of Proverbs was designed as a schoolbook for the instruction of young men and not for children is revealed in the caution against the loose woman (Proverbs 5) and in other sayings. Much of the first nine chapters of the book is an invitation to learning. The term *my child* in the book is both a literal and a conventional term. Both father and mother offer parental counsel in Proverbs; but in addition the schoolmaster served as "father" to the "children," who were his students.

Notice that wisdom is portrayed as a woman. Dame Stupidity is set over against Dame Wisdom in the proverbs. For example, "The foolish woman is loud" (Proverbs 9:13). However, Dame Wisdom has set up seven pillars and has built her house (Proverbs 9:1). Dame Wisdom invites young men to

> lay aside immaturity, and live,
> and walk in the way of insight.
> (Proverbs 9:6)

This statement expresses the central thrust of the proverbs. In the Book of Proverbs we have the best single source for discovering the values of the people of ancient Israel.

The proverbs are not arranged according to any particular themes. Life is pictured as the supreme good; and the good life included an abundance of friends, a house full of children, and sufficient possessions to carry one safely through any difficulty. Notice that none of the proverbs expresses any hope for life beyond the grave. Life is simply a pilgrimage of the wise and the foolish. The wise are blessed with a good life; and the foolish come to a sad, disgraceful end.

The book contains different forms of proverbs. Many have a single balanced line. The one-line proverb exhibits parallelism: Two halves are balanced in antithesis or synonymy, with some having a synthetic parallelism.

A proverb with antithetical parallelism sets opposites over against each other:

> A false balance is an abomination
>> to the LORD,
>> but an accurate weight is his delight.
>>> (Proverbs 11:1)

A variation of this type is what is often called a "Better-proverb" or excluding proverb, such as,

> Better is a dinner of vegetables where love is
>> than a fatted ox and hatred with it.
>>> (Proverbs 15:17)

Notice that the saying does not attempt to determine the better of two things but rather announces that one is good and its opposite is bad.

The second form of proverb uses what is called synonymous parallelism. In this form an astute observation is reinforced by repetition of the essential point in different words. Here is an example:

> Hear, my child, your father's instruction,
>> and do not reject your mother's teaching;
>> for they are a fair garland for your head,
>> and pendants for your neck.
>>> (Proverbs 1:8-9)

A progressive proverb builds on an earlier idea and advances beyond two similar notions to an entirely new concept:

> The beginning of wisdom is this: Get wisdom,
>> and whatever else you get, get insight.
>>> (Proverbs 4:7)

We find in the following example a variant of the progressive proverb in which the second line is essential for the meaning of the proverb:

> Like a war club, a sword, or a sharp arrow
>> is one who bears false witness
>> against a neighbor.
>>> (Proverbs 25:18)

The numerical proverb is another type:

> Three things are stately in their stride;
>> four are stately in their gait.
>>> (Proverbs 30:29)

Another type of proverb lists comparable phenomena without the numerical heightening that is found in Proverbs 30:18-19, 21-23, 29-31:

> Four things on earth are small,
>> yet they are exceedingly wise.
>>> (Proverbs 30:24)

In addition to a number of different types of proverbs, the Book of Proverbs contains three types of wisdom: clan, court, and theological. Clan wisdom was aimed toward helping people master life. This type of wisdom seeks to explain nature and human relationships with practical reasoning. Most of the proverbs seem to have come out of a clan setting. Some of the proverbs came from the royal court, however. These proverbs had a limited audience. Their wisdom was aimed at potential rulers and at advisors to persons in power.

The third type is theological wisdom, which differs radically from the clan and court wisdom proverbs. Its intention was to provide education for everyone, regardless of social standing. These proverbs accomplish this task through the use of dialogue and admonition. Underlying this form is religious teaching regarding proper conduct.

The most distinctive feature of theological wisdom is the emphasis on "fear of the LORD." In Proverbs the "fear of the LORD" means purely and simply that which every person owes God. Without a proper relationship with God, no one can possibly attain enough wisdom to be called wise. Proverbs 1 holds up the "fear of the LORD" as the beginning of wisdom:

> The fear of the LORD is the
>> beginning of knowledge;
>> fools despise wisdom and instruction.
>>> (Proverbs 1:7)

In teaching the proverbs, we must keep in mind that "the fear of the LORD" is the key to living the right kind of life. May these ancient words of wisdom guide you now and in the years to come.

Adapted from *Adult Bible Studies Teaching Helps,* Summer 1990 (Copyright © 1990 by Graded Press); pages 3–4.

Chapter One

THE BEGINNING OF KNOWLEDGE

PURPOSE

To help us discover that faith in God leads to true wisdom and to moral living

BIBLE PASSAGE

Proverbs 1:1-9, 20-23
Background: Proverbs 1

> ### CORE VERSE
> The fear of the LORD is the
> beginning of knowledge;
> fools despise wisdom and instruction.
> (Proverbs 1:7)

LESSON OUTLINE

1. Introduce Our Need
2. Examine Our Source
3. Establish the Purpose
4. Acquire Skills
5. Discover Fear
6. Consider Homemade Wisdom
7. Put Wisdom to Work
8. Respond to the Call

GET READY

Have a chalkboard and chalk or large pieces of paper and markers available for use during the session.

Be sure Bibles and copies of the student book are available for the class members.

LESSON PLAN

1 Introduce our Need

One topic most people like to talk about is the weather. Once I participated in a ministerial exchange with a pastor from England. For six weeks I was in Nailsea; and Reverend Brian Dams pastored the church I served in Washington, Iowa.

When my wife and I returned home, we spent two days with Reverend Dams and his wife. They shared their feelings about the hot weather they had experienced. The temperature reached one hundred degrees, and Mr. and Mrs. Dams really suffered from the heat. As a result, the Dams became quite conscious of the weather. Each evening they watched the news on television in order to hear the weather report for the next day. Reverend Dams commented about the extensive details that weather forecasters provide in the United States as compared to forecasters in the United Kingdom.

In the UK, the weatherperson gives a brief and simple explanation of the conditions that exist in the atmosphere and then indicates what the weather will be the following day. In the US, the weatherperson gives extensive details. He or she talks about all the fronts, points out the direction in which they are moving, and explains what lies behind them and ahead of them. The weatherperson gives seemingly endless attention to the causes and effects of the weather pattern before finally telling what the weather conditions will be the next day.

I like the Book of Proverbs because it, like the weather forecaster in the UK, deals with life in basic, simple terms. When I read from the Book of Proverbs, I am not confronted with a lot of detailed explanations. Each statement is quite clear and deals with specific experiences. I do not have to read a lot of complicated material before reaching the predictions. There is no room for questions or speculation when the truth is stated in the form of a proverb. Proverbs are forceful, accurate, and to the point.

A proverb is a statement of two ideas, either in comparison or in contrast. One of my favorites is,

> There is gold, and abundance of costly stones;
> but the lips informed by knowledge are a
> precious jewel.
>
> (Proverbs 20:15)

The two contrasting statements are a prediction of where true value is to be found.

The proverbs are quite explicit and exact in their explanations of life and of human behavior. The direct and explicit style of the Book of Proverbs is vastly different from the way modern persons discuss human behavior.

The vast majority of modern ethical positions vacillate somewhere between extreme ethical relativism and radical absolutism. That is, persons in our society constantly move between being circumstantial in their decision making and following a rigid set of do's and don'ts. This vacillation is in marked contrast to the clear, direct approach the Book of Proverbs uses.

Ask: *Do you think our society has become too permissive? If so, why has this happened? Do you think our society should have a strict code of morality? Why or why not?*

On pages 6–7 in the student book, the writer discusses an incident in which he thought he had secured a boat. Soon, however, he discovered that the rope had come loose and that the boat had drifted off. Many fishermen have had such an experience. For example, one day a friend and I were fishing; and we decided to drop anchor. The wind was from the south, and we wanted to locate our boat off a certain point of land. I tossed the anchor over the side, and we settled down to cast for fish. I soon noticed that our position had changed in relation to the point of land. I thought perhaps the anchor did not reach bottom, and we were drifting. I looked over the side, and the water was clear enough to see the anchor on the bottom of the lake. The rope was stretched upward. All appeared to be well. We continued to fish, but a little later I noticed that our position had changed again. Our boat had drifted quite some distance from where we wanted to be. This time I looked over the side, but the anchor was not there. I looked back to the south. Sure enough, our anchor was back there. The rope reached upward, but it was not attached to the boat.

I had thrown the anchor over, but I had not tied it to the boat. At first everything appeared to be tied together. In reality, however, I was not anchored to anything.

Living by appearances is a way of life with many people. As long as things appear to be what they want them to be, they think life is all right. Once I went shopping for some furniture. The salesperson said, "This is the best wood you can buy." I questioned him about the kind of wood he said it was. He referred to it as walnut, but I thought it was oak. After closer inspection I said, "Isn't this a veneer?" His reply was, "No, it is a solid piece." I said, "We can tell by looking at the edge." When I looked at the edge, what appeared to be the real thing was only paper glued to particle board.

I have reservations about living by appearances. When you invest money in something that is supposed to be the real thing, you want your money's worth. The purpose of this session is to help us discover the message of the Book of Proverbs that faith in God leads to true wisdom and to moral living.

2 Examine Our Source

Proverbs 1:1. This verse identifies the source of the Book of Proverbs as "Solomon son of David, king of Israel." In spite of this identification, however, we cannot be certain that Solomon is the sole source of the Book of Proverbs. In the ancient Near East it was common to attribute literary works to a king. Someone may have credited the Book of Proverbs to Solomon as an honor. Or, Proverbs may have been attributed to Solomon in order to give these writings more status and credibility. Or, the book may bear Solomon's name in recognition of his great wisdom (1 Kings 3:1-14). Or, the Book of Proverbs may have been associated with Solomon to indicate that these writings are not "common" in any way. The quality of the material included in the book is such that it seems appropriate to associate it with a person of Solomon's stature. How direct an association Solomon had with the material in the Book of Proverbs will probably always remain a mystery.

3 Establish the Purpose

Verses 2-6. These verses state the purpose of the book. These proverbs were written to help people strengthen their character. Some of the verbs in these verses stress this purpose. The Book of Proverbs was written so that people may "learn . . . about wisdom" (verse 2), "gain . . . instruction" (verse 3), "hear" (verse 5), "gain in learning" (verse 5), "acquire skill" (verse 5), and "understand" (verse 6). Thus, the readers are to acquire specific abilities that will enable them to handle the basic affairs of life in a way that will lead to the best results.

Proverbs is, therefore, a practical book. It provides guidelines that can help people manage their lives in the best possible way. The result will not be an accumulation of facts and data. Instead, the result will be the development of judgment and the ability to plan and manage one's life more effectively.

Encourage the class members to discuss the purpose of education in our nation's school systems. Ask: ***Does education have a purpose beyond instilling facts and figures in students' minds? Should the primary purpose of education be to help individuals learn to manage life and to develop meaningful values? What are some ways in which your education helped prepare you for life?***

4 Acquire Skills

One of the personal skills the student of Proverbs is to acquire is "prudence" (verse 4). We rarely use the word *prudence*. I wonder how I would feel if someone described me as prudent. I would have to stop and think about the meaning of the word: "Wise in handling practical matters; exercising good judgment or common sense." Being prudent usually means that one has the ability to plan ahead and to plot a course of action.

When I attended a workshop on time management, one of the disciplines the instructors sought to convey was planning. I have also learned from experience that if I know all the items I need to take with me when I leave home, I will not have to make a return trip to get the one item I forgot. Prudence is an important asset in managing the common affairs of life.

We also need to clarify the meaning of the word *simple* (verse 4). Many scholars believe the word refers to uninformed youth. This proverb is addressing persons who are maturing, those who have yet to acquire the wisdom of ordering and managing their lives.

Studying these proverbs can help the student acquire the ability to understand "the words of the wise and their riddles" (verse 6). The riddles referred to are not those we might view as games. These "riddles" are a serious matter. We sometimes say that life is like a puzzle, confusing and hard to understand. If we can exercise wisdom, however, we will be able to solve the riddle and to uncover the meaning.

5 Discover Fear

Verse 7. "The fear of the LORD is the beginning of knowledge" (Proverbs 1:7).

Ask: ***Are you familiar with this verse of Scripture? If so, what is your interpretation of its meaning?*** *Fear*, as the word is used in verse 7, does not mean being frightened. Nor does the proverb refer to an overwhelming desire to run and hide or to escape. My family and I have spent a few vacations in the mountains. We have ventured out on some of the footpaths that lead to the highest parts. At such times I have had the frightened kind of fear. At other times, however, I have had the fear of wonderment and awe. Fear, as it is used in Proverbs 1:7, is fear in the sense of respect and honor. For example, if someone handed me an extremely valuable object, I would treat it with fear—not the fear of breaking it but the fear that comes with sensing its value.

Chapter 6 of the Book of Isaiah gives us a good example of the fear of God. Isaiah had a vision of the immensity and greatness of God. This experience was so overwhelming that it changed Isaiah's life. From that time on, he answered the call of God and was sent forth to speak for God.

Ask: ***What does it feel like to fear God? What is the difference between "reverent fear" and "frightened fear"?*** (*"Reverent fear" will draw us toward God in wonder, love, praise, and worship. "Frightened fear" will draw us away from God and call forth our feelings of guilt and inadequacy.*)

When we play board games, we always start at the first square. That is the beginning of the game. When Proverbs 1:7 says that "the fear of the LORD is the beginning of knowledge," the word *beginning* is quite significant. The writer is saying more than that knowledge begins with reverence for God.

When a contractor builds a house, he or she digs down into the earth and pours the footings for the foundation. This process is the beginning of construction. Laying the foundation is the first thing that happens in terms of chronology. Laying the foundation is more than just the first task that is performed, however. Everything else in the entire project depends on the foundation. The whole structure rests on it. This "beginning" means much more than just being first in the order of things. "Beginning" in this context means being first in importance and being essential to the total project. Without "the fear of the LORD" there is no knowledge, no wisdom, and no basis for moral living.

6 Consider Homemade Wisdom

Verses 8-9. According to the writer of the Book of Proverbs, wisdom begins at home. Instruction and discipline from parents is not to be viewed as a burden but as a beautiful preparation for one's future (Proverbs 1:8-9).

Research has shown us that the home continues to be the primary source of education for children and young people. While the schools and the church play a large part in supplying the factual knowledge students need and in affecting their attitudes, the home is still primary during the formative years. The encouragement and stimulation offered in the home provide an invaluable foundation for the total educational experience of the individual.

In the time when the Book of Proverbs was written, the parents were a living link between the wisdom of the past and the needs of the children. The children could learn through trial and error, but they would be wise to listen to their parents' instruction instead. Parents are still responsible for instructing their children in the kind of common sense wisdom necessary for daily living. The child who views the rules and words of caution offered by his or her parents as "a fair garland" instead of as an imposition is truly wise.

Ask: *How has the wisdom received in your childhood home affected your present life?* (*Most class members will remember decision-making occasions when the advice of parents has been recalled.*)

7 Put Wisdom to Work

Verses 20-23. Beginning in verse 20, the writer of Proverbs 1 employs an unusual image: He personifies wisdom. Wisdom is given human form and lifts her voice so as to be heard. She takes her place in the mainstream of life.

Wisdom's message is quite clear in terms of being understandable as well as in terms of being loud enough to be heard. Wisdom calls for repentance. She wonders how long the simple and the scoffers will ignore her appeal to them. They continue to ignore her, and she proclaims that there is a limit to her patience. A calamity will befall them, and it will be sudden and overwhelming. "They shall eat the fruit of their way" (verse 31). Wisdom does not mete out the punishment; it is the inevitable result of the actions of those who have ignored her.

Personification of an idea or concept is a quite effective method of teaching. We have one of the greatest examples of this truth in Jesus Christ. The Gospel of John declares that "the Word became flesh" (John 1:14). God's love for humankind was expressed and enveloped in the life of Jesus Christ. If we have faith in someone, we believe in him or her—we believe in the validity of the idea he or she embodies. Through Christ we receive insight into the teachings of God.

The good news of Jesus Christ is a timeless message of wisdom. The insight and enlightenment it provides relate to all ages. We are not merely to sit back passively and absorb it, however. We must constantly strive to understand the good news and to apply it in terms that the church has not used previously. We cannot simply rely on the same forms that Christians have used in the past. We must have wisdom—Christ's wisdom—to function effectively as a church.

8 Respond to the Call

When I was a child, I lived in a neighborhood where four other boys and I played together. When it was time for supper, our parents would call us by name. The calls would ring throughout the whole block and would reach our ears wherever we happened to be. All of us learned to respond to those calls promptly.

Ask: *How is the wisdom of Christ being expressed in the church today? How are we responding to its call?*

To close the session, pray the following prayer:

Dear God, help us to have ears that hear your call to wisdom. When we have heard, lead us to respond positively and to turn to a way of life that will enable us to find fulfillment. We thank you for sharing wisdom with us, especially in the life of Jesus Christ, in whose name we pray. Amen.

TRY ANOTHER METHOD

To help members become familiar with the type of material found in the Book of Proverbs, form several small groups of two or three persons. Assign a chapter of Proverbs to each group and have them read the chapter and choose several favorite verses to share with the total group.

If you have some artists in the group, have them draw a picture of wisdom as a woman based on Proverbs 1:20-33.

Take some time to let members share bits of wisdom they learned from their parents when they were children.

Chapter Two

THE PRIORITY OF WISDOM

PURPOSE

To challenge us to embrace the ways of wisdom that lead to abundant living

BIBLE PASSAGE

Proverbs 4:1-13
Background: Proverbs 4

> **CORE VERSE**
> The beginning of wisdom is this:
> Get wisdom,
> and whatever else you get, get insight.
> (Proverbs 4:7)

LESSON OUTLINE

1. Introduce Our Need
2. Discuss Formation of Life
3. Examine a Parent's Request
4. Claim Our Heritage

GET READY

Read Proverbs 4, Chapter 2 in the student book, and the material in this teacher book.

Have a chalkboard and chalk or large pieces of paper and markers available for use during the session.

LESSON PLAN

1 Introduce Our Need

I attended Morningside College in Sioux City, Iowa, back in the 1950's. College campuses were rather calm in that decade. In fact, our era has been labeled apathetic. We did not have any causes, any discontent, or any unrest—just the task of getting an education and a job. World War II was past. The veterans had graduated. The Korean War had turned into a peace-keeping action. The civil rights movement and the war in Vietnam were still ahead of us.

Even without the stress and pressures of earlier and later generations, however, I managed to gain some lasting impressions from my college experiences. I minored in psychology. One of the required courses was Child Psychology 101. I was not at all interested in understanding children. When the professor handed out a packet filled with questions concerning the behavior of children, I cringed at the prospect of having to learn the subject.

I struggled with many of the questions and answers. I had to do a lot of research, and I had to discuss the meanings and intentions of the questions with other students to gain the slightest comprehension of the subject. Much to my delight, however, in the midst of the struggle, I came across one question that had an obvious answer. The question was, "Why is it vital that the years of childhood have a good beginning?" I proceeded to answer the question without giving any authoritative source. I stated that beginnings are important because the habits that we form early in our lives are long lasting. The beginnings create the original qualities of life for the child. Furthermore, to correct or to reform bad beginnings is quite difficult.

The first two verses of Proverbs 4 stress just such beginnings. A father is concerned with the formative years of his children. The father is urging the children to acquire those qualities that will sustain them as they grow and mature, to embrace the ways of wisdom. He wants his children to begin life with habits that will have lasting value and result in abundant living.

An incident in the life of William Jennings Bryan illustrates the influence of the formative years. When Bryan first began practicing law, he represented a client who was to receive money that Bryan recovered in a lawsuit. After Bryan had collected the money for his client, he put it in his safe until the client could come for it. When someone asked Bryan why he did not use the money for his own needs, he answered that early in life he learned the dangers of using something that belonged to others.

2 Discuss Formation of Life

Ask: *Can you recall any instructions you received in your formative years that had a profound influence on you? If so, why have they influenced you? Are children today receiving an adequate foundation early in their lives? Why or why not? How are parents, schools, and churches helping children get a good start in life?* (*You may want to form small groups so all members will have an opportunity to share their experiences. A time limit on answers or elimination of one or two questions would also be appropriate.*)

On page 15 in the student book, the writer comments on the trouble parents have in helping children establish solid beginnings. He points out that often parents encounter difficulties because of the double standards they erect. One of the most common of these double standards is revealed when parents bring their children to church but do not attend themselves. Perhaps the parents go to a local restaurant for coffee or go back home to read the newspaper. They return to church in time to find a place to park in the drive so their child can make it to the car without the parents having to meet them at the church door. Transporting a child to and from church requires time and energy, but it is only a minor part of setting the child's "spiritual foundation" in place.

Parents must learn and grow in order to be able to pass valuable qualities of life on to their children. Virtues acquired at the beginning of life last only as long as they are nurtured. If parents do not sustain them, they have nothing left to pass on to their children; and they must transport the children to a place where others will nurture the children. The double standard can be expressed in the sentence, "I want you to learn what I failed to maintain."

The student book writer's second observation concerns the lack of authority of the church. The writer comments that this matter is compounded by the diversity of thought and belief that exists within the church. The absence of a single authority causes some perplexity among the laity and clergy.

Since the church does not speak with one voice, how can parents find clear, decisive statements on moral issues to transmit to their children? We cannot avoid struggling with this difficult issue. We should not condemn the church for this situation, however. The church's diversity is one of its most valuable assets. We should appreciate this diversity and not consider it a weakness.

Ask: *Would you rather have the church give the ultimate answers to life's issues, or would you prefer that the church provide guidance and help as you search for your own answers? Why?*

3 Examine a Parent's Bequest

As I read Proverbs 4, I think of a parent writing a letter to a child. The parent has a deep longing to do all within his power to persuade the child to live a good life. The parent shares three bits of advice in this letter, apparently hoping to point the child in the right direction. The letter stresses the value of wisdom, urges the child to proceed along the right pathway, and advises the child to remain steadfast once wisdom is acquired.

Proverbs 4:1-5. The significant thought in these verses is the importance of "transmission." In each generation the home is where the transmission of wisdom from one generation to the next occurs. The parents are the ones who bequeath wisdom to the children, just as they have received wisdom from their parents. In the Book of Proverbs all fathers are "Solomons" in their roles as sages and teachers. The father refers to his own experience—when he was the only child and received instructions from his parents. The autobiographical information strengthens the father's teachings. We can assume that all previous generations received wisdom in the same fashion.

Verse 5 contains the strongest appeal a parent can make regarding wisdom. The parent stresses that the child must never forget wisdom. The tone of the admonition is one of encouragement, not criticism.

Invite the class members to comment on how we

present the Christian faith to youth. Ask: *Do we take a negative approach and emphasize what young people should not do? Or do we encourage them in the faith and make them want to "get wisdom"? What can the church do to make the Christian faith appealing to youth? Is there a difference between saying "Don't forget, you have to go to Sunday school" and "I hear the youth group is doing some great service projects"?* (*You may want to assign one or two class members to discover the specifics about your church's youth ministry and to suggest ways your class can be supportive.*)

Verses 6-9. In order to stress the great benefit of wisdom, the writer uses marriage as a metaphor. He personifies wisdom as a wife and places great value on all the benefits she will provide her husband if he will love her and not forsake her. Wisdom, like a prized wife, will exalt and honor her husband and bestow a garland and crown, symbols of victory and authority.

Verses 10-19. Most of us know what it is like to be driving down the highway, cruising along at sixty-five miles per hour. The flow of traffic is normal and orderly, and everyone assumes there will be no interruption. Then just ahead you catch sight of a flashing light in the shape of an arrow. You are immediately aware that the flow of traffic is going to be rerouted due to repair work. As you approach the flashing sign, the lanes merge into one. Before you looms an array of inverted cones marking the path for the traffic. Finding your way becomes a puzzle. Sometimes it is hard to distinguish which is the right path. As long as you obey all the traffic signs, however, you will not have any difficulty. When the father warns his son about the route he must follow, the phrases read like road signs: "Do not enter" (verse 14), "do not walk" (verse 14), "avoid" (verse 15a), "turn away from" (verse 15c).

Those who follow in the way of wisdom and stay on the right path will find the pathway wide and void of obstacles. This pathway is well lighted and easy to see and leads to abundant living.

The writer describes the nature of the wicked who depart from wisdom. Those who plot and commit evil become insatiable for crime. They are unable to sleep "unless they have done wrong" (verse 16). They become intoxicated with the desire for violence.

On page 18 in the student book, the writer shares the testimony of criminologists and prison counselors. These people say that the more violence some criminals commit, the more they desire. This understanding, if true, raises many questions about the destiny of humankind. Is it inevitable that nations that pursue the path of violence and terrorism will multiply their efforts? Is the only way to deal with this problem to exterminate evildoers from the face of the earth?

Ask the class members to share their feelings about criminals and the treatment they should receive. Ask: *Should our communities emphasize reformatories or penitentiaries? Should our efforts be directed toward rehabilitation or toward punishment? How do we close down the road leading to wickedness?* (*You may want to remind class members that the Social Principles of one mainline denomination state, "In the love of Christ, who came to save those who are lost and vulnerable, we urge the creation of a genuinely new system for the care and restoration of victims, offenders, criminal justice officials, and the community as a whole. . . . Through God's transforming power, restorative justice seeks to repair the damage, right the wrong, and bring healing to all involved, including the victim, the offender, the families, and the community."[1]*)

Verses 20-27. The class members are probably familiar with Paul's image of the body. That is, Paul says that the body is composed of many parts; yet all of them are united in harmony (1 Corinthians 12:14-26). Just as Paul sought to present an image of wholeness, the poet declares that wisdom must control all the parts of one's being.

The first part of the anatomy the writer of Proverbs refers to is the heart (verse 23a). The heart is both an ancient and a contemporary symbol. Today bumper stickers use the heart as a symbol of love. The writer of Proverbs speaks of the heart in a more profound way, however. The Hebrews believed that the heart was the seat of thinking, the deepest source of consciousness. The *Good News Bible: The Bible in Today's English Version* (*TEV*) translates verse 23, "Be careful how you think; your life is shaped by your thoughts."

This passage of Scripture is further enhanced by the reference to the "springs of life" flowing from the heart. Imagine a stream flowing from deep within the ground. Think of a cold, clear stream of water that flows without ceasing. Wisdom comes from the depths of one's life in the same way, and it is inexhaustible.

Wisdom should also purify one's speech (verse 24). The writer does not say that wisdom will provide eloquence, but wisdom should make a person's speech pure and truthful. Eyes that look straight ahead (verse 25) will serve as evidence of the truthfulness of one's speech. We are still inclined to view those who look us straight in the eye as honest.

In the closing verses the writer uses the imagery of paths a second time (verses 26-27). This time he says that if a person is aware of the path he or she is following, then the right path will be easily followed. If you have ever walked through a forest, you know that the trail that is well used is easy to follow. To stray from this pathway may place a hiker in grave danger. The writer declares that wisdom is a pathway that is well used, and a person walking this path should not depart from it.

4 Claim Our Heritage

Three particularly important thoughts come to mind after reading Proverbs 4. We need (1) to remember the beginning of our faith, (2) to take stock of its effects on our lives, and (3) to share the faith with others.

The Iowa Annual Conference of The United Methodist Church maintains a community for older adults at Fort Dodge, Iowa. In the archives room a pulpit, an altar, and a railing are placed in a corner. I was curious about these items being there, since the room was not a chapel. When I inquired, I learned that one of the residents had made his commitment to Christ at this altar rail. Some time back the church building was dismantled, and this person salvaged these furnishings. When he moved into Friendship Haven, he brought the furnishings with him. This contribution to the archives was the way he remembered the beginning of his faith.

The father in Proverbs 4 recalls how he came to receive the foundation of his life—through the teachings of his parents when he was the only child in the home. If we could question the writer, he would probably be able to tell us about many moments when he was being taught.

Encourage the class members to talk about how they first became Christians. Ask: *Where did you become a Christian? Did a special person influence your decision? Was a book particularly meaningful to you? Is there one event that you can identify and claim as the beginning of the shaping of your faith? What have been some of the milestones along the way?*

Just as the writer of Proverbs details the rewards that wisdom bestows on the practitioner, we should be able to describe the way our faith has affected our lives.

Some people think that our faith guarantees us riches. Others think that it will enable us to escape the discomforts of life. Both views are wrong, of course; but how are we to declare the true values of the faith?

We can testify to the power for abundant living that our faith has given us. I always find it rewarding to conduct a service, whether it be a funeral or a wedding, for people whose faith has been important to their lives.

I usually ask for personal thoughts to share in the service that will express some of the elements of their faith. Without fail, there is a vital and meaningful message to offer that enhances the whole service. These messages are similar in spirit to the message of the writer of Proverbs who affirms the gifts that wisdom bestows on people. As followers of Christ, we are called to articulate the personal gifts that have come into our lives as a result of our faith.

Faith is not something we keep to ourselves. Because of the joy and strength that it brings to our lives, we want to share it. We want others to receive abundant life.

Let's return to the path that the writer speaks of in Proverbs 4. Some hikers who are coming along the path may find an obstacle in the path that is dangerous. As they make their way around the obstacle and continue on their journey, they encounter hikers coming from the other direction. They share their experience and warn the hikers what they will be coming to on the trail. After the second group of hikers pass by the obstacle, they meet a third group; and they share the warning. Soon the word has spread up and down the trail, and everyone is alerted to the obstacle and told about keeping to the safe path.

For the sake of everyone, for the love we have for God, we will pass the words of eternal life on to others we meet along our spiritual journey.

Ask: *What role should the church play in assisting persons on their spiritual journeys? How does evangelism enter into this task? Is it enough to have an altar call, or are we bound to share in a personal way with others about our faith? Is Christian education fulfilling its duties in transmitting the faith to people starting out on their journeys of faith?* (*You may want to form several small groups to discuss one or two of these questions and then to report to the total class.*)

To close the session, ask the class members to think about what they have learned during the session. Invite them to comment on the highlights of the discussions. Then ask: *What have you gained from the session?* When all who wish to do so have answered, have a few moments of silence and meditation. Close by asking the class members to pray sentence prayers that reflect the meaning of this lesson. These prayers can be prayers of thanksgiving or prayers for guidance in fulfilling the duty to help others on their journeys of faith.

[1]From *The Book of Discipline of The United Methodist Church, 2000* (Copyright © 2000 by The United Methodist Publishing House); page 119.

TRY ANOTHER METHOD

Locate any official statements of your denomination concerning criminals and the treatment they should receive. Discuss the statements in light of the events of September 11, 2001. How has our nation responded to those responsible for those events? How are Christians called to respond?

Supply pens and paper and ask class members to write brief letters to their children or the children in your church offering them words of wisdom about the "right paths" to follow in life.

Chapter Three

THE VALUE OF WISDOM

PURPOSE

To help us develop a sincere affection for wisdom as an expression of God's creativity

BIBLE PASSAGE

Proverbs 8:22-36
Background: Proverbs 8

CORE VERSE
Hear instruction and be wise,
and do not neglect it.
(Proverbs 8:33)

LESSON OUTLINE

1. Introduce Our Need
2. Talk About Personifying Wisdom
3. Discover a Style
4. Examine Wisdom's Prominence and Origin
5. Discuss Evidence of Prominence
6. Explore God's Wonders

GET READY

Read Proverbs 8, Chapter 3 in the student book, and the material in this teacher book.

Have a chalkboard and chalk or large pieces of paper and markers available for use during the session.

LESSON PLAN

1 Introduce Our Need

It is Sunday, and we have come to the second hymn of the worship service. The organist plays a short introduction, and then the congregation joins in singing the first verse. We continue and come to the third verse. I glance at the center of the chancel to make sure the child-size chair is there. I check the microphone hanging around my neck, making sure it is hooked in place. As we begin the last verse, I close my hymnal and place it in the hymnal rack; push a button that turns on my microphone; and move to the center of the chancel.

Glancing over the congregation, I see some adults squeezing back in their pews to make room for children to pass in front of them. In other parts of the congregation, adults are leaning forward toward the chancel with an expression of encouragement on their faces. One child walks timidly down the center aisle. Another child runs down a side aisle. Children are coming forward from every direction, singly or in small groups. By the time the hymn is finished, I am seated in the child-size chair, looking into the faces of children seated on the floor in front of me.

You have probably observed such an event, or something like it, on many occasions. Perhaps you have had to move aside to allow a child to pass in front of you. Or you may be a parent who gives or has given your child the courage to walk down that long aisle in front of all those people. Things look a lot different from my position as pastor, however; I must come up with a word to share with these expectant children that will have a connection to the rest of the service.

Sometimes I have the feeling that all that would really be necessary would be just to spend time with the children.

The congregation could see how beautiful the young people are and could enjoy their youth and enthusiasm. Yet if the children's time becomes only a display for the adults, I am guilty of failing to fulfill my responsibilities as pastor. That is, I am guilty of simply using the children to entertain the rest of the congregation.

The time spent with the children is an important part of worship. The hymns, Scripture, sermon, and prayers used during the worship service normally have a common theme. Presenting the theme to the children requires using terms and images that are familiar to them. Working out such a talk is a real challenge.

2 Talk About Personifying Wisdom

I think my experience is comparable to that of the person who personified wisdom as God's companion during Creation. The writer of Proverbs 8 had an idea that he wanted to convey. Rather than stating the idea in stale, bland terms, he gave us a brilliantly painted picture. He presented wisdom as a woman and gave her a place of prominence in God's presence and a share in God's mighty act of Creation.

As we explore the writer's ability to portray wisdom so vividly, we will fulfill the purpose of this lesson, which is to develop a sincere affection for wisdom as an expression of God's creativity.

Ask the class members: *Can you recall an illustration that increased your understanding of the faith?* (*The class members may recall something a pastor said in a sermon or a comment by a Sunday school teacher or friend. Encourage the class members to distinguish between the illustration and the idea or truth it conveys.*)

3 Discover a Style

One evening I arrived home late. Out of habit, I turned on the television set. I did not find anything of special interest, so I settled for a program that I would at least be comfortable watching. As I listened to the dialogue, the conversation began to sound familiar; I had heard it or something like it before. The words reminded me of some of Mark Twain's writings, but the story line was unfamiliar. When the program ended and the credits were listed, my suspicions were confirmed. The drama was "Adam and Eve" by Twain.

A common "tone" is present in most of Mark Twain's writings. Recognizing it is no different than recognizing a friend's voice on the telephone. Mark Twain found a distinctive style and used it effectively in telling his stories.

The writer of Proverbs also has a style with which we may become familiar. Quite often we find him writing in terms of personification. That is, in order to convey his ideas, the writer gives them a personality. On pages 25–26 in the student book, the writer explores two contrasting personifications the writer of Proverbs uses. One is the adulteress (Proverbs 7). The other is wisdom (Proverbs 8). Ask the class members to review these pages in the student book. Then invite them to read and compare Proverbs 7:10-23 and Proverbs 8:1-12. Notice how the writer skillfully employs personification. Point out in particular Proverbs 7:10-12; 8:8, 20.

The writer of Proverbs used this style to declare the concept of wisdom in a way that would enable other people to understand it. The writer had looked at the world and discovered something about it. He wanted to share this discovery, so he came up with a lovely way of describing his discovery. He created a reality from what wonderment revealed to him. That reality includes the beautiful story we have in Proverbs 8. Through his words we are able to see the wonder of wisdom and the role it has in God's creativity.

Ask: *What arouses feelings of wonder in your life? Is wonder something you feel now, or is it something that you recall from your childhood? Is wonderment a meaningful way to relate to life, or is it better to understand our world in strictly rational terms? How does wonderment relate to your feelings about God?* (*The class members should recall the feelings of wonderment they have or have had about life. Being able to experience something and be excited is wonderment. For example, wonderment may arise from visiting a building in England that was constructed many centuries ago. Even though one knows many facts about the place and the events surrounding it, one can still have a sense of wonderment that goes beyond the facts and makes them come alive.*)

4 Examine Wisdom's Prominence and Origin

The writer of Proverbs wanted to assure us of the prominence of wisdom. Thus he said that wisdom was in existence before anything else (Proverbs 8:22-23). God created wisdom "first of his acts of long ago." The exact date of origin is incidental for the writer, since wisdom was created "before the beginning of the earth." He could not even imagine a time when wisdom did not exist.

We may have some friendships like that. With some of our friends, we may look back and feel that we have always been friends. We find it hard to imagine that there was a time in our lives when we did not have a special friendly feeling toward each other. The writer is saying that wisdom has always been a companion to God—before anything else was.

The writer of Proverbs also emphasizes the prominence of wisdom by mentioning its longevity. Wisdom is the oldest; therefore, it has seniority over all things.

I grew up in a neighborhood where all the children were boys. I happened to be the oldest. At an early age the role of authority was bestowed on me. When it came to choosing up sides, I was the one who made the first selection. When there had to be a leader, I would be given that awesome task. Just because I was the oldest member of the group, I had the greatest responsibility for leadership.

The culture that produced the Book of Proverbs bestowed status on the aged. Even though our society emphasizes youth and many products designed to preserve one's youthful appearance are sold, we still grant a special status to older adults. We recognize that their experience has great value. Since it is common practice to attribute importance to something that has existed a long time, the writer says wisdom has great significance because of its long existence.

Scholars make various distinctions regarding the origin of wisdom. God may have possessed wisdom as a personal trait and employed it in the acts of Creation. God may have created wisdom from a source other than himself, that is, out of nothing. Wisdom may have been born from God. The exact means by which wisdom came into existence is not important. The writer wants us to realize that wisdom is an entity separate from God and that wisdom was manifested by God before anything else was. Regardless of its origin, wisdom had a significant role in the drama of Creation. This role gives a unique identity to wisdom and elevates it to the highest pinnacle of importance in relationship to all other creatures.

5 Discuss Evidence of Prominence

After establishing the pre-existence of wisdom, the writer reinforces his point by listing the events that followed the creation of wisdom. As each event is listed, the writer links it with wisdom, thus affirming wisdom's prior existence. As each event occurs, wisdom is placed in the midst of the event. The writer piles up the "long agoes" and "befores" with this listing. He does not credit wisdom with Creation. Yet by giving the panoramic vision of all that transpired, the longevity of wisdom is magnified; and the role of wisdom is accentuated.

When my wife and I worshiped at a church I served as pastor many years ago, I enjoyed seeing old friends and renewing those ties. Our friends invariably referred to events in a way that made it clear that it had been quite some time since I served that parish. As we discussed our families, the small children who were part of my memory were now described as young adults. Many of them were married, and their children were running down the aisles of the church. When the morning was over, I was quite conscious of how long ago I was there and what I was a part of "when."

The writer of Proverbs refers to the long ago time "when" wisdom was created. "When" was before any of the many moments of Creation. Each act of Creation was spectacular, but wisdom was before all of them. Wisdom was present and involved during the spectacle.

People have many different opinions about Creation. Their discussions usually focus on whether the biblical account in Genesis describes the "how" of Creation. Some of the class members may wish to get into a debate over this question as a result of reading Proverbs 8:22-31. Rather than yield to that temptation, however, ask the class members to consider the student book writer's statement on page 27 that "we certainly can embrace the theological affirmation central to the Creation story, the idea that the world and our existence in it have meaning and value only because of God." The "how" is not as important as the "Who."

Such an affirmation does not mean we should pass over the writer of Proverbs' description of the steps of Creation, however. The writer's words are a beautiful expression of his faith in the God from whom comes all creation.

Symbols represent something greater than themselves. They cause us to look to the reality they represent. The Quakers place virtually no emphasis on furnishings and decorations in their meeting houses. Instead, they emphasize silence and speaking only when the Spirit prompts them. The sparseness of furnishings and the abundance of silence are not a denial of symbols, however. The sparseness and silence are symbols—symbols that I have greatly cherished when I have worshiped with Quakers or visited a historic meeting house. The symbol is the reality of the wonderment we experience. When we have an inspiring symbol like the words of Proverbs 8, we should treasure it, not ignore it.

The symbolic beauty of this account of Creation captures our attention and appreciation. This account has a wonderful structure and orderliness. The sage establishes the presence of wisdom before there was a source of water. No depths or springs existed (Proverbs 8:24). With our understanding that God created out of chaotic waters (Genesis 1:1-2), the only thing that could have existed before these waters was nothing. Yet the writer of Proverbs says that when there was nothing, there was wisdom.

Proverbs 8:25-26 is a clear example of orderliness. The writer begins with the mountains and looks backward to the hills, the fields, the soil. He concludes that wisdom was present during the creation of the smallest parts of the universe as well as of the most magnificent. Before even the insignificant particles of soil came into existence, wisdom presided.

Proverbs 8:27-28 mentions the outer limits that encircle the earth—the sky and the sea. Wisdom was there when the heavens were established and the depths were placed in their boundaries. This activity completed the limits and put the finishing touches on creation. God "assigned" the limits of the sea and marked the "foundations of the earth" (8:29). Wisdom was always present.

The writer described the world as he understood it. At some point in time the world was brought into being—from the largest to the smallest, from the highest to the deepest. The existence of these things is measured in terms of time and space. In the midst of this existence wisdom dwells—and dwelt before any part of it came into being. Wisdom is given prominence in view of her pre-existence and presence while God was fashioning all his handiwork. She is pictured as being delightful to God and as rejoicing in his world and his ultimate creation, human beings (Proverbs 8:30-31).

A twofold meaning is present in the Hebrew word the writer uses to describe wisdom in Proverbs 8:30. One meaning is that wisdom was a craftsman, a workman. Wisdom had a hand in fashioning creation. The other meaning of the word is suggestive of a child at play. While God was involved in Creation, wisdom was enjoying the spectacle. Both meanings fit the context of the passage.

Wisdom commends her ways to the dwellers of the earth because her ways are rewarding (Proverbs 8:32-36). Those who neglect the ways of wisdom will succumb to death and emptiness.

6 Explore God's Wonders

Our study of this passage from Proverbs reminds us of the need to be open to different forms of speech that can enhance and deepen our understanding of God's wonders. On page 28 in the student book, the writer says that "we must be open to new forms of divine revelation." God cannot be captured in just a few terms or pictures.

A little child was drawing a picture in Sunday school. An adult happened by and asked the child what she was drawing. She said, "God." "But no one knows what God looks like," advised the adult. The child confidently responded, "They will when I'm finished."

This anecdote helps us to realize that sometimes we think we have said all that can be said about God. We must be like the writer of Proverbs, however. We must be open to new visions and images of God.

We must be willing to share our new understandings about God with others as well. We must be willing to talk about God. One man told me that religion is a personal matter, and he indicated that it is something one should not discuss. Such a view implies that one's faith is something that should be kept private. Expressing our views and listening to those of others is a way of growing, however. Our faith is nurtured when we are active in the community of faith, not when we are withdrawn and alienated.

Ask: *Do you feel the need to discover new concepts about God? Are you open to talking about God? Do you feel comfortable expressing your views about the nature of God? Why or why not? Do you find it hard to know what to say? In what ways does the passage of Scripture we have explored help you express your beliefs about God?* (*Class members will have varying answers to these questions. Remind them that as they explore the content of the Bible, they will gain an ever greater appreciation for the beauty of the various faith expressions of the writers and an increasing ability to express their own faith commitment.*)

Close the session with the following prayer:

Dear God, open our souls that we may receive new visions of your nature. Help us to open our lips that we may speak about you in more meaningful ways. Help us speak as your disciples, that we may share our faith with others and, in sharing, grow. In Jesus' name we pray. Amen.

TRY ANOTHER METHOD

Prior to the session, ask several class members to search for new ways of expressing faith commitment. They will want to look for these ways in art books, in television or radio programs, in newspapers and magazines, in books, in people they meet, in the Bible, or in nature. Perhaps they might want to try their hand at creating an expression of their faith commitment by designing a banner, writing a poem, or using one of their other talents. Be sure to have a display table in the classroom to share their creations at the session or to allow sufficient time during the session to share the creations with the total group.

Chapter Four

LESSONS FROM LIFE

PURPOSE

To recognize that the biblical writer is giving moral instruction so that we may lead a life conforming to God's will

BIBLE PASSAGE

Proverbs 22:1-16

CORE VERSE

A good name is to be chosen rather than great riches,
and favor is better than silver or gold.

(Proverbs 22:1)

LESSON OUTLINE

1. Introduce Our Need
2. Look at the Text
3. Examine Personal Qualities
4. Discuss the Value of Caution
5. Talk About Economic Reality
6. Consider the Humor of Laziness

GET READY

Read Proverbs 22:1-16, Chapter 4 in the student book, and the material in this teacher book.

Have a chalkboard and chalk or large pieces of paper and markers available for use during the session.

LESSON PLAN

1 Introduce Our Need

When I was in junior high school, I looked forward to my fifth-period class every day. This period was my music class, or more specifically, chorus. I enjoyed music and singing, and the school I attended had a fine program. The room was spacious and well suited for chorus. The chairs were arranged in a large horseshoe shape so all the choir members could see the director.

Our music teacher was a fine instructor. She gave individual attention to each choir member whenever necessary. If someone needed a little encouragement in singing out, she would coax the volume out of the person. If someone was disrupting the proceedings, that student would also receive immediate attention. The teacher kept a ruler on top of the piano. Many times we would hear a crack as she rose from her piano stool and struck the ruler on top of the piano. Then with a stare, she captured the troublemaker's attention.

As her cold stare thawed, our teacher would gently lay her ruler down; but instead of returning to the music score, she would step from behind the piano and begin to moralize. These lectures could be quite extensive, but they were not judgmental. She spoke to us about our behavior and about our worth. She said that each of us had some unique quality that was quite special and valuable.

Although some of my classmates thought her lectures were merely amusing and entertaining, most of us found them beneficial. When we came out of the session, we had enjoyed the period of singing; but we also had a better attitude about ourselves and others.

Once I was attending a local service club meeting. The high school basketball coach was the speaker. His team had just completed a successful season, and the coach told us about the preparation he and the team members had made. Early on, the team members discussed their goals with one another and made a strong commitment to them. As practice continued, the players were drilled in the fundamentals of the game and rehearsed all the necessary movements. In addition, the coach encouraged the team members to have a winning attitude. He gave lectures, put up posters, and did everything he could to reinforce the players' winning attitude. He knew that if they focused on their goals in the right way, they would have what they needed to go out and win. This program formed the young people into a winning team and molded them into individuals who received a great deal of respect from the community. They were not only a winning team but were also successful as human beings.

Many programs are available that are designed to help people develop a winning attitude. These programs advise participants to establish a correct thought and constantly to reinforce it. The program leaders say that as a result, the participants' lives will be steered in the right direction.

We human beings are creatures. We must acquire our identities. If we are going to be musicians, we have to learn the appropriate skills. If we want to be athletes, we must learn how to play the game. If we desire to grow up to be saints, we must learn what is involved and then practice it. On page 35 in the student book, the writer says that "good character is not inherited; it must be learned."

The writer of Proverbs is giving moral instructions so that we (the students) may lead a life that conforms to God's will. My music teacher not only instructed me in music, she implanted a right way of life in my mind. The members of that basketball team not only learned to play the game well, they developed the proper attitude with which to play the game. In order to conform to God's will, we must be taught.

Ask the class members about their experiences of moral growth. Ask: *Who or what has helped you develop and lead a moral life? How important were the teachings you received about having a right attitude and good habits?*

2 Look at the Text

If you are looking for an orderly, progressive development of thought in Proverbs 22, you will be disappointed. This chapter is a collection of materials that have great value, but they do not necessarily link together.

When my family and I move, it means getting everything we own gathered and boxed up so it can be loaded on a moving van. As we pack, we know exactly where most things are. We go to our closets and find our clothes hanging in their proper places. We go to the bookshelves and find the books arranged there in a logical order.

Some of the drawers we open are a hodgepodge of articles, however. I find myself rummaging through the contents, intrigued with all the items and sensing how important they are. Yet if I am required to explain just why any specific article is there or where it will be placed in our new home, I am at a loss. So I dump each drawer's contents in a box. I know that we will sort through the boxes later and find a place for all the items in our new home.

Proverbs 22 is an assortment of verses that fall together just because they happened to be in the same "drawer." They are not arranged in an orderly fashion. With a little effort, however, we can sort them into some categories. We will arrange the material in the following way:

I.   Personal Qualities (verses 1, 4, 6, 11)
II. The Value of Caution (verses 3, 5)
III. Economic Reality (verses 2, 7, 8, 9, 16)
IV. The Humor of Laziness (verse 13)

3 Examine Personal Qualities

Proverbs 22:1 places great value in a good name. The mere mention of some people's name can bring a smile to our faces. Once I met someone whose occupation caused me to think we might have a common acquaintance. When I spoke the name of the person I had in mind, he immediately began to talk about what a fine person our mutual friend is. A name can bear the character and reputation of a person.

Proverbs 22:1 teaches that a good name, a good reputation, is more valuable than wealth. Ask: *How high on your scale of values do you rank a good reputation? Does our society still place value on character, or are persons judged by their credit ratings or their popularity? Why?*

Verse 4 mentions another personal quality: humility and fear of God. Humility is the quality of being humble. The humble person lacks pride and is modest. In terms of relationships, those who are humble are aware of their own shortcomings. As a result, they do not judge others too harshly. Such persons are also aware of their relationship to God. They "fear" (have reverence for) God because they know they are creatures and he is the Creator.

Verse 11 refers to two more personal qualities. The writer points out that there are advantages to having a pure heart and gracious speech. Even a king will be the friend of a person who has these attributes. In routine conversations I occasionally hear a person mentioned for no other reason than his or her goodness. Such a person is always warm and caring and is usually treated well in return.

Ask the class members to think of someone they know whom they respect. Ask: *How would you describe this person? Do the words you use to describe him or her reflect purity and graciousness?*

Verse 6 also relates to personal qualities indirectly. Children usually follow the pathway that is set for them by the training they receive at home. Having a wholesome early life benefits persons as they grow older. We acquire our personal identity through the things we learn, and the home is one of the most basic sources of education.

4 Discuss the Value of Caution

Two verses in Proverbs 22 encourage caution: verses 3 and 5. In verse 3, a prudent person is described as one who plans ahead and tries to use good judgment. The writer contrasts such a person to a simple person. The simple person takes no thought of what lies ahead and simply goes forward without heeding any warnings. In verse 5, thorns and snares get in the way of the perverse, those who are wrongly self-willed or stubborn. Those who guard themselves and proceed with caution, by contrast, are able to keep far away from such traps.

Through modern technology we now have the means to predict various dangers. For example, weather forecasts have become quite accurate. If a storm is brewing halfway across the continent and it may have some effect on our part of the country, the forecaster warns us. When a blizzard or a hurricane is on the way, it is a blessing to know in advance and to have some time to prepare. Many persons immediately check their supply of food and then rush to the supermarket.

My wife grew up on a farm in the central part of Iowa before so much information about the weather was readily available. Her family did not have a lot of advance notice about the weather, but they were weather wise. Whenever the weather looked threatening, her father would take the family down into the storm cellar.

Yet in spite of the early warnings and the availability of shelter of all kinds, some people still ignore dangerous weather. For example, they refuse to leave their coastal homes during hurricanes. These people seem determined to try to stand up against the elements whatever the cost might be. They fail to demonstrate the prudence the writer of Proverbs calls for.

Ask: *What are some prudent actions that our nation as a whole or you as an individual have taken recently? Is it prudent to maintain safeguards against terrorism? How should we react to warnings about various hazardous products? What about wearing seat belts?*

5 Talk About Economic Reality

Sometimes our image of God is that of a being who is quite impartial, almost without feelings. When grave injustices occur, we wonder why God permits them to take place. We want a God who is just and who is concerned about the rights and wrongs of everything that happens. Sometimes it seems that God is more like a judge, occupying the bench in a courtroom and doing nothing but listening.

The verses of Proverbs 22 dealing with economic reality (2, 7, 8, 9, 16) do not present this type of God, however. The God we see here is one who is definitely on the side of the poor and oppressed. The writer leaves no doubt as to the position God takes.

> The rich rule over the poor,
>   and the borrower is the slave of the
>   lender.
> (Proverbs 22:7)

On pages 36–37 in the student book, the writer treats this observation as the typical condition of life and speaks about the grave hardship this economic situation can bring into the life of a family. We can be casual about this matter and say it is just the way it is. When issues erupt from business dealings that cause hardship and anguish in people's lives, however, it is hard to say something is "just good business."

This verse is doing more than making an economic observation. The writer is making a statement filled with feelings about the conditions that exist for people who have to borrow. When people borrow, they become a slave to the lender. The borrower must fulfill all the terms of the agreement and sometimes is called to risk all for the sake of the loan. We should not treat this observation casually. The writer's comments are a perceptive evaluation of the harshness of life.

The writer of Proverbs makes it clear that God is concerned about the poor and the oppressed (Proverbs 22:2, 8-9, 16). The writer is issuing a call for acts of kindness toward the poor, as well as saying that God forbids mistreatment of the poor:

> Whoever sows injustice will reap calamity,
> and the rod of anger will fail.
> (Proverbs 22:8)

Read aloud the following section of the Social Principles of one mainline denomination:

E) *Poverty.*—In spite of general affluence in the industrialized nations, the majority of persons in the world live in poverty. In order to provide basic needs such as food, clothing, shelter, education, health care, and other necessities, ways must be found to share more equitably the resources of the world. Increasing technology, when accompanied by exploitative economic practices, impoverishes many persons and makes poverty self-perpetuating. Therefore, we do not hold poor people morally responsible for their economic state. To begin to alleviate poverty, we support such policies as: adequate income maintenance, quality education, decent housing, job training, meaningful employment opportunities, adequate medical and hospital care, and humanization and radical revisions of welfare programs.[1]

Compare this statement with the verses of Proverbs 22 regarding economic issues.

Ask: *How do you think God feels about the way prosperous church members relate to the poor and disadvantaged? How can we offer help in finding solutions to some of the problems of world poverty?*

6 Consider the Humor of Laziness

The lazy person has always been the object of ridicule and disdain. The implicit charge is that such people are negligent, irresponsible, and lacking in character.

We may laugh at Proverbs 22:13 when it states,

> The lazy person says, "There is a lion outside!
> I shall be killed in the streets!"

Yet maybe we should have sympathy for such a person. If our fear becomes great enough, our imagination will enlarge danger to unreal proportions. A person may have phobias of all sorts, including being afraid of driving in traffic, of coming in contact with germs, or of being in a crowd. The statement about the lion may sound laughable, but I wonder if perhaps it reflects some fears that have been magnified. When persons are "put down" long and often enough, they are bound to become afraid of life in general. Rather than admit that, they express their fear in other ways, which we may misinterpret as laziness.

Living faithfully, like any skill, takes practice. Practice means that we learn to do something the right way, and then we rehearse that way until it becomes natural. The writer of Proverbs presents rules for righteous living. The readers are expected to follow in those ways until they make them their own. When they do, they will be leading lives that conform to God's will.

To close the session, lead the class members in the following prayer:

Dear God, forgive us for permitting our skills in faithful living to become so rusty. Help us to practice so that we might acquire more polished and established habits of the Christian life. In the name of Jesus Christ our Lord, we pray. Amen.

[1] From *The Book of Discipline of The United Methodist Church, 2000* (Copyright © 2000 by The United Methodist Publishing House); page 115.

TRY ANOTHER METHOD

Illustrate the section on laziness with strips from the cartoons "Beetle Bailey" or "Mama." Beetle is notorious for finding ways to escape anything that looks like work and for sleeping as much as possible in the army. Mama's youngest son is known for being too lazy to hold a job and for finding excuses for not getting out of bed.

The suggested closing prayer speaks of our skills in faithful living. Take some time before or following the prayer to list skills class members may want to practice during the coming week.

Chapter Five

PROVERBS IN PICTURES

PURPOSE

To help us realize that we can draw important moral values and spiritual insight from carefully observing human behavior and from examining the realm of nature

BIBLE PASSAGE

Proverbs 30:18-33
Background: Proverbs 30

> ### CORE VERSE
> If you have been foolish, exalting yourself,
>   or if you have been devising evil,
>   put your hand on your mouth.
> (Proverbs 30:32))

LESSON OUTLINE

1. Introduce Our Need
2. Discuss Expressions of Awe
3. Examine the Beauty of Motion
4. Consider Some Mysteries of Life
5. Explore Majestic Decorum and Arrogance
6. Recognize Wisdom in Nature

GET READY

Read Proverbs 30, Chapter 5 in the student book, and the material in this teacher book.

Have a chalkboard and chalk or large pieces of paper and markers available for use during the session.

If possible, have some large pictures or posters of animals on hand.

Have copies of a hymnal available so the class members can read and sing "All Things Bright and Beautiful."

LESSON PLAN

1 Introduce Our Need

Once we had a Bassett Hound for a pet. Our children would dress her up, put hats on her, and adorn her with glasses. Then the children would take pictures of her. The photos left us thinking how much like a human being that dog was. She thrived on the attention and seemed to try to look her best during the photo sessions.

If possible, bring some pictures or posters of animals to the session. Show them to the class members. Then ask the class members to share their impressions. Ask: *What causes you to feel a sense of wonder about these pictures? What are some of your other feelings and thoughts when you look at such pictures?* (*The class members may express some humor, or they may make some quite serious and meaningful remarks. Something in the pictures may leave the class members with a deeper sense of the ultimate meaning of life.*)

When the class members have finished their discussion, point out the purpose of this lesson: to help us realize that we can draw important moral values and spiritual insight from carefully observing human behavior and the realm of nature.

Each week many programs about animals appear on television. In most cases the makers of these programs carry their complex equipment to a site where a certain creature can be photographed. After studying the surroundings for a long time, the camera operators decide how to conceal themselves in order not to frighten the animals. Then these people spend many tedious hours, sometimes waiting, other times in the excitement of a brief moment, just to capture a scene that represents the life of the creature.

When these films appear on television, they greatly entertain and enrich the audience. If that were not the case, no one would watch; and advertisers would not pay for the cost of the programs. In many cases these programs are the only means children have of seeing animals and the surroundings in which they live.

Through such vivid portrayals coming into our living rooms, we have an opportunity to gain a deeper appreciation of God's world. The writer of Proverbs 30 was also an observer of the world around him and spoke of the wonders of God's creation with a sense of awe.

In Proverbs 30:18, the writer expresses both a sense of wonder and a lack of understanding. He has looked on things in the world of nature and is left with questions and amazement.

My wife and I like to take hikes. Occasionally, we come across some of God's lovely creatures and are filled with awe. When we see a deer, for example, we stop just to watch. The creature will often pause too and gaze at us for a long time, giving us the opportunity to behold the beauty of its head and eyes. Then it will turn and bound away. While my wife and I must have a path that is well marked and cleared, this creature can move through the tangle and jumble of the trees at a loping pace without hesitation. Every time we see a deer, we comment about the wonder of God's creation.

Some people have the idea that a person must have special training in order to go out into nature and view God's creatures. Other people think that they must have an exciting adventure, or the experience will not be worthwhile. However, several of my friends and I, who have no background in the study of nature, like to find a small wooded area and to spend a great deal of time slowly walking around and being amazed at each creature we see. The outing is as exciting as it would be if we were standing on the edge of the African continent and beholding its amazing creatures.

We all have the ability to be filled with the wonder and amazement expressed by the writer of Proverbs 30 if we give ourselves the opportunity.

2 Discuss Expressions of Awe

In a parish I once served, we had friends who would call late in the evening and ask, "Is the coffee pot on?" If it was not, it soon would be; and these friends would arrive at our front door shortly thereafter. We then sat around the kitchen table and enjoyed talking together.

The husband was a good storyteller; and he invariably began by saying, "You know, I just can't understand . . ." Then he would go on with his tale. Sometimes he would include two or three things that puzzled him. After reading Proverbs 30, I could not help but think of my friend.

The way my friend began his stories was quite intriguing. If something about the story was amazing, he mentioned that fact at the beginning. Doing so gave the listener some indication of what to look for. This approach gave coherence to everything that followed. The writer of Proverbs 30 does that. He gives the conclusion of his observations before he tells the story. This practice is almost like giving the punch line to a joke before one tells the joke itself. The writer has looked at the world around him, particularly the creatures; and he is left with a sense of awe.

All the writer's observations are nicely categorized. The three or four in each group have a common theme. This approach indicates that the writer had an orderly mind and that he carefully organized his material. Although the conclusions are not the sort of information produced by scientists today, his observations are valid.

Many of us fail to "see" some of the things we look at day after day. Yet when someone calls them to our attention, they can take on new meaning. We were on a vacation trip one summer and stopped in a small park for a break from driving. For a little exercise we walked down a trail and came to an opening in the trees that looked out on a panoramic scene. I was just going to suggest that we should get back to the car and be on our way when our youngest child said, "It looks just like a picture card." I was struck by his observation. I took a good look; and sure enough, no one could have captured the awe of the view before us in any better terms.

The writer of Proverbs gives us a personal impression of the world as he saw it through eyes of wonder and awe. We can ponder his words and draw some of our own conclusions.

3 Examine the Beauty of Motion

In Proverbs 30:18-19, the writer expresses his sense of wonder at the beauty of motion. He stands in awe at the sight of an eagle aloft, a snake moving in wavelike fashion, and a ship slipping through the ocean depths.

Sometimes when driving along, I catch sight of a bird high in the sky, just floating. The bird does not even have to move a wing to continue flying. Its wings are outstretched, and it dips and rises as it glides through space in lovely circular motion. The sheer beauty of flight leaves me filled with amazement.

Although the snake is a creature with a bad image, the writer of Proverbs appreciates it for the unique means of mobility it has. By curling and uncurling its body, the snake is able to undulate wherever it wishes to go. Once I was in the visitors' center of a state park when the ranger was feeding some snakes. He took the snakes out of their container and allowed me to hold one of them. I got up enough nerve to let the snake coil around my arm, and I noted with amazement the wonderful structure of its body and the strength of its grip on my arm.

I remember quite well also the beautiful scene when the tall ships sailed into New York Harbor on July 4, 1976. They looked magnificent. I have always loved to stand on the shore of a lake and watch the sailing vessels, whether they be large or small. The way they play with the wind is marvelous.

If the writer of Proverbs 30 could have looked at the wonders of the modern world, he probably would have included hot air balloons on his list of the beauty of motion. Personally, I am filled with wonder when I take an airplane flight. The plane is motionless on the runway. Then with full throttle it rapidly makes its way down the pavement and into the air. I never have been quite able to understand how such a heavy object can seemingly float above the clouds.

Ask: *What are some objects of motion that amaze you?* (*The class members will have various answers to this question. Some of the members may mention creatures from the world of nature; but others may mention mechanical objects, such as a race car.*) Then ask: *What gives you the sense of wonder? Is it the means of the motion? Is it the rhythm, or is it the power or grace?*

4 Consider Some Mysteries of Life

The fourth item that creates wonder and amazement in the writer of Proverbs 30:19 is the sensual attraction of a man for a young woman. Unfortunately, this mystery of life that is the basis of family life and the guarantee of the propagation of humanity has become degraded in books, magazines, television shows, and so forth. Too often the makers of soap operas and films find their plots in the subject of adultery (verse 20). The fact that some people find adultery entertaining is evidence of how far moral standards have deteriorated in our society.

Society, however, has not given in entirely to this situation. God created us all with a sense of right and wrong. Sooner or later, people's consciences react when they are guilty of betrayal and infidelity. I have seen persons filled with great remorse for the wrongs they have done. They often turn to the church for counsel and support.

Verses 21-23 discuss another of life's mysteries—situations among humankind that can have a volcanic effect on the earth. These verses have to do with reversals. The writer's perception is remarkable. When a slave becomes king, the nation not only trembles, it is unable to bear up. A slave, who is used to taking orders, does not have the skills needed to rule well. When a fool is filled with food, he or she will almost assuredly display unbecoming behavior. When a woman who is unloved (hateful) becomes married, she is incapable of the love of the marriage bond. When a maid takes the place of her mistress in marriage, she is not capable of genuine love because she probably came to the position through unworthy means.

In each instance a person of inferior rank is elevated to high rank. In a way, the writer's words do not ring true with our concept of democracy. Americans believe that anyone can become president of this country. No person's rank in life makes him or her unfit for higher privileges. We know that many people have started out from humble circumstances but have been able to rise to be the dominant force in a community or organization. So we would not subscribe to the writer's words without reservation.

On the other hand, the writer does speak perceptively of the problems that come when those who are unworthy of higher privileges attain them. Persons who have spent a great deal of time being unlovable may find it difficult to make the transition to being loving. Individuals who have been ruled over for their entire lifetime may create chaos if given the responsibility of ruling. I have seen persons elected to public office who had no qualifications for the job other than popularity. They not only did nothing positive themselves, they made a shambles of what their predecessors had accomplished.

Ask: *Do you see any evidence in our culture of assigning persons to one social level and forbidding them to move above it? If so, what? Are we truly a nation that gives opportunities to all people without reservation? Are there times when we must discriminate against certain persons?*

Another mystery of life for the writer of Proverbs 30 is the evidence that size is not always an indication of might, especially when wisdom is involved. In verses 24-28, the writer refers to four small creatures that perform great feats. Ants gather food during the summer months to see them through the winter. Badgers have the uncanny ability to construct their homes from stone. Locusts display a detailed system of rank and organization. Lizards are quite commonplace, but they have access to the palaces of kings.

God's "lesser" creatures have amazing qualities. These creatures exhibit some of the greatest designs in all creation. The ant has developed a complicated system of community. The badger has a unique dwelling place. The locust has a form of government, and the lizard is a social climber.

Size does not always indicate might, particularly in the community of nations. A nation's effectiveness is not always determined by its material resources. Many small nations have displayed a great deal of wisdom in the way they administer their affairs. For example, the tiny country of England grew to become the British commonwealth of nations.

5 Explore Majestic Decorum and Arrogance

In verses 29-31, the writer again takes note of God's creatures. The manner of their stride is striking. This characteristic reveals the stateliness of the nature of these creatures: the lion, the strutting cock, and the he-goat. The fourth example is from the world of humans: a king before his people. In each of these cases the subject walks with a majesty that displays self-assurance and demands respect.

All people use body language. The way we position our bodies when sitting, working, and so forth communicates something that others may be able to understand. The amazing thing about body language is that we are usually unaware that we are saying anything. Yet sometimes we are saying more than we want to. Sometimes a strut can reveal arrogance and self-pride rather than healthy self-esteem.

Verses 32-33 are an admonition to guard against arrogance and wickedness. The arrogant and the wicked should be silent in view of their wrongdoing. The writer makes his point in a poetic way by using three analogies. A lot of action only sours milk. Hitting someone in the nose only produces a bloody nose. Planning evil only gets a person into trouble. All in all, such action is futile.

6 Recognize Wisdom in Nature

We are blessed with sages who continue to be aware of the great wisdom we can gain from observing the world of nature. These persons are the people who continue to remind us of how precious our environment is. They warn us that we must care for it in order to exist ourselves.

Environmentalists stand in awe and wonder at the flight of a bird, at the mobility of a snake, and at the power of the wind to drive a sail. We who have been given dominance over the earth have treated it badly. We are like the slave made king, the fool well fed, the unloved suddenly granted the bond of marriage. Lest humanity strut in a majestic but arrogant manner, the environmentalist is warning us to cease our wicked ways.

Read the following statement from the Social Principles of a mainline denomination to the class members:

All creation is the Lord's, and we are responsible for the ways in which we use and abuse it. Water, air, soil, minerals, energy resources, plants, animal life, and space are to be valued and conserved because they are God's creation and not solely because they are useful to human beings. Therefore, let us recognize the responsibility of the church and its members to place a high priority on changes in economic, political, social, and technological lifestyles to support a more ecologically equitable and sustainable world leading to a higher quality of life for all of God's creation.[1]

Then ask: *How do you feel about this statement? What specific actions could our class take to "support a more ecologically equitable and sustainable world leading to a higher quality of life for all of God's creation"?* (*Perhaps your class could start a recycling collection center or join with other community groups who are working to improve and protect the environment.*)

To close the session, ask the class members to meditate on the words of "All Things Bright and Beautiful." Then ask the members to join in singing the hymn.

---

[1] From *The Book of Discipline of The United Methodist Church, 2000* (Copyright © 2000 by The United Methodist Publishing House); page 96.

TRY ANOTHER METHOD

Open your session by playing a few minutes of a nature video, one that shows the habits of a particular bird or animal. Then ask a class member to read Proverbs 30:18-19, 24-33 aloud.

If your class members are not familiar with the hymn "All Things Bright and Beautiful," substitute "This Is My Father's World" or "I Sing the Almighty Power of God."

If you have an artist in the group, ask him or her to illustrate Proverbs 30:20-33. Display the appropriate drawings as you discuss each section of the Lesson Outline.